NATIONAL GEOGRAPHIC OUR WORLD

The North Wind and the Sun

Based on an Aesop's Fable
by Jill Korey O'Sullivan

NATIONAL GEOGRAPHIC LEARNING | CENGAGE Learning

T0349939

One day the Sun and the North Wind
see a man. It is a cold day.

The man is wearing boots, jeans,
a sweater, and a coat.

Wind says, "I am strong! I can blow the man's coat off."

Sun says, "Really? Show me."

Wind blows.

"It is windy, but the man is still wearing his coat," says Sun.

"I can blow it off!" says Wind.

Wind blows and blows. It is very cold and windy. But the man's coat does not blow off.

5

Sun says, "Watch me do it!"

Wind laughs and says, "You can't blow like me. You can't do it!"

Sun shines on the man.

It is sunny and hot.

Sun shines and shines.

It is very hot.

The man is hot.

He takes off his coat.

Wind says, "You are very smart, Sun."

Sun says, "Thank you, Wind."

Facts About Temperature

Is it hot today? Is it cold? A **thermometer** can tell you!
A thermometer measures **temperature**.
Temperature is how hot or cold something is.

These things are cold.

snowman

ice cream

ice

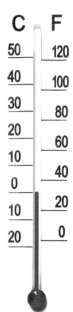

These things are hot.

soup

the sun

fire

boiling water

What other things are hot or cold?

Fun with Weather and Clothes

Write the words for the clothes.

boots   coat   jeans   sweater

coat

Draw clothes for each kind of weather.

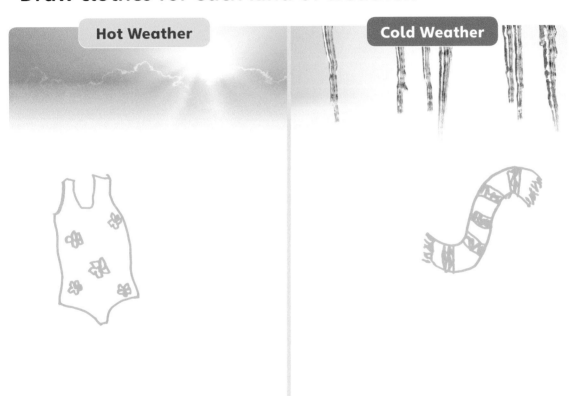

Hot Weather

Cold Weather

Glossary

blows

laughs

man

shines

smart

watch